ideals®

THANKSGIVING

Thy beauty, O God, is upon us, autumn splendor everywhere—days lucid with vision or dim with mist, haze and smothered sunshine; nights wistful with summer memories. The trees are touched with ripe, mellow colors, and the leaves begin to fall and flutter away. The birds are going south, following a viewless path like the homing instinct in the soul of man.

Lord, we thank Thee for beauty. Let our thankfulness be the flower of thoughtfulness and our prayer the fruit of joy. Help us, O God, to make the life of man as lovely as the world in which he lives, the brotherliness of humanity equal to the beauty of nature. Amen.

Joseph Fort Newton

ISBN 0-8249-1014-1 350

IDEALS—Vol. 39, No. 7 November MCMLXXXII IDEALS (ISSN 0019-137X) is published eight times a year, February, March, April, June, August, September, November, December by IDEALS PUBLISHING CORPORATION, 11315 Watertown Plank Road, Milwaukee, Wis. 53226 Second class postage paid at Milwaukee, Wisconsin. Copyright © MCMLXXXII by IDEALS PUBLISHING CORPORATION. POSTMASTER: Send address changes to Ideals, Post Office Box 2100, Milwaukee, Wis. 53201 All rights reserved. Title IDEALS registered U.S. Patent Office. Published simultaneously in Canada.

ONE YEAR SUBSCRIPTION—eight consecutive issues as published—$15.95 TWO YEAR SUBSCRIPTION—sixteen consecutive issues as published—$27.95 SINGLE ISSUE—$3.50

Publisher, James A. Kuse
Editor/Ideals, Colleen Callahan Gonring
Associate Editor, Linda Robinson
Production Manager, Mark Brunner
Photographic Editor, Gerald Koser
Copy Editor, Barbara Nevid
Art Editor, Duane Weaver

New England in the Fall

Helen E. Middleton

When the hillsides blaze with glory
  And we hear the loon's thin call,
Let us go to old New England,
  To New England in the fall.

Winding roads are made for travel
  By the mountains and the sea;
Skies are blue and air is bracing;
  Autumn flings her tapestry,

Scarlet, saffron, smoky purple.
  And by some clear river's mouth,
We may glimpse, with awe and wonder,
  Arrowed wild geese heading south.

Though we roam the wide world over
  Following adventure's thrall,
Nowhere holds more brilliant beauty
  Than New England in the fall!

Familiar scenes of autumn
Are new—yet centuries old.

On patchwork sky, the fall winds write
    A tracery in blue on white,
While mountains wear designer clothes—
    Red maple cloak, gold aspen hose.
The night sky moves without a sound
    To fling a million stars around,
And harvest moon, in full-spread shine,
    Shows bumper crops on field and vine.

A Thousand Blessings

Alice Leedy Mason

Familiar sounds of autumn
Have stories to be told

Of school bells ringing loud and long,
    Of children's voices raised in song.
They tell of wild geese sailing high
    (Theirs but to go, not question why).
November winds now promise rain.
    The cat purrs by the hearth again.
Home folks recall old times, old ways,
    While chancel choirs sing hymns of praise.

Familiar thoughts of autumn
A thousand blessings hold.

The earth keeps changing, sometimes green;
    Sometimes it has a golden sheen.
One grows accustomed to the way
    Bright colors crown an autumn day.
How good it is that God still cares;
    He fills His world with sumptuous wares.
The heart at last with wisdom sings
    Of beauty in familiar things.

The Indiscreet Chrysanthemums

Dorothy Bettencourt Elfstrom

Defiant of November's sober skies,
They flaunt their colors in the frosty air.
With gaiety and mischief in their eyes
They scoff at Old Man Winter's icy stare.

He's standing in the wing of Nature's stage,
Impatient to begin his ruthless role.
Accompanied by winds that moan and rage,
He muses of his wicked, nearing goal.

"Those flowers shall lose their heads,"
   they hear him growl,
And though they realize their timely fate
And hear the north wind's angry, answering howl,
Today they live—tomorrow is too late!

Laurie English Dawson

Laurie English Dawson has always loved poetry but did not do any writing until after the age of fifty. For years, many stories were in her mind about the places and people she knew. When she did begin to write them in verse, the "words seemed to come alive." Mrs. Dawson was born in Maury County near Mount Pleasant, Tennessee. She grew up in a large happy family on a farm surrounded by beautiful hills and valleys. She has been a widow for over forty years and, since her retirement, has moved back to the county of her birth. She remains active doing church work and teaching a Sunday School class. Mrs. Dawson is very pleased to have had many of her poems published in Ideals.

A Thanksgiving Picture

I'd like to see Thanksgiving Day
In colors on a screen,
A day of feasting, sharing, giving,
A joyful, friendly scene.

I'd like to see the countryside
A land where all are free
And opportunity holding out
A hand to you and me.

I'd like to see the hearts of men
Give thanks with humble love
For all the bounty we receive
From the Giver up above.

An Old-Fashioned Thanksgiving

Nothing makes Thanksgiving dear to the heart
Like old-fashioned kitchens where cooking's an art.

Singing teakettles and fat pumpkin pies
So spicy and fragrant and just the right size,

An old-fashioned rocker, great red pepper strings
To brighten the hearth where the old cricket sings,

The fat roasted turkey with dressing and spice,
The plums and the pickles and everything nice—

Nothing keeps Thanksgiving dear to the heart
Like old-fashioned kitchens where cooking's an art.

Everyday Thanks

For newborn mornings, soft and still,
And stars you see from frozen hill,

For splendor of the stars at night
And a woman's face by candlelight,

For dusty attics full of toys,
For fishing poles and freckled boys,

For telegrams that bring good news,
For understanding another's views,

For sunlight on a small boy's face
And little girls with simple grace,

For waiting arms, homecoming bliss—
My thanks each day for all of this.

The Thanksgiving Season

The Thanksgiving season is in every way
Just the right time for a nice holiday;
It comes in the fall when the crops are laid by,
When the soft harvest moon seems to lighten the sky.

The Thanksgiving season is in every way
Just the right time for parties so gay,
For football and feasting and bright nippy weather
When families and friends can all get together.

The Thanksgiving season seems extra nice
When kitchens are sunny and smelling of spice,
When the fat pumpkins grow ripe on the vine
And are made into pies so tasty and fine.

Thanksgiving season seems in every way
Just the right time to bow and to pray,
To give thanks for bounty that we have to spare,
For love and for friendship we have to share.

Thanksgiving on the Farm

I like to spend Thanksgiving Day
On the farm where I used to play.
I like the look on Grandpa's face
When he bows his head and says a grace;
He's thankful for the barns of hay,
For all the blessings of the day,
For health and friends and loved ones near,
For happiness throughout the year.

Thanksgiving Day

On the eve of golden autumn
When November days are crisp and clear,
Etched upon my heart are memories
Of childhood's happy yesteryears.

I hear the village church bell ringing
As home folks gather there to pray
Thanking God for every blessing
On a glorious Thanksgiving Day.

After church the homeward journey
O'er the hill and through the woods,
Out across the searing meadow,
There an ancient farmhouse stood.

Woodsmoke drifted from the chimney,
Pungent-sweet upon the air,
Extending to all a hearty welcome
From the dear ones living there.

Fragrant aroma from a laden table
Prepared by loving hands to share,
Each head bowed in humble reverence
In sincere and thankful prayer.

Like a chest of precious jewels
Locked within this heart of mine,
Cherished memories never leave me,
Linger on until the end of time.

Julia A. Bowman

Autumn Season

Flora Elliott

I like the autumn season
When Thanksgiving Day draws near
With air so crisp and biting
And sky so blue and clear.

The harvest safely gathered
Before winter winds will blow;
No need for any hunger
When the earth is banked with snow.

The kitchen smells of pickles
And whets my appetite
With jars of apple jelly
And mincemeat flavored right.

The heaping apple barrels
Now array the cellar floor
With fruit so red and rosy,
Sweet and mellow to the core.

Wild geese are winging southward
In a slow and graceful vee;
The squirrel at last is resting
In his hollow in the tree.

All the earth is now retiring;
She has given of her part,
And man looks back on summer
With a warm and grateful heart.

It gives a peaceful feeling,
At this closing of the year,
To know our toil was worthwhile,
And now leisure days are here.

I always feel Thanksgiving
Is the turning of the key;
One door is shut behind us,
But another opens free.

Manifold Blessings

The golden harvesttime has come again
And is replete with summer's bounteous yield;
We voice thanksgiving in a glad refrain;
We kneel in reverence to our source and shield.

Remembering the joyful copious days,
The blessings manifold, through storm or strife,
In humble faith and gratitude we praise
Our mighty Lord, the King of love and life.

A steadfast hope and gladness He imparts;
Each act of strength comes from His guiding hand;
We offer thanks for true and valiant hearts
That strive to give us peace in every land.

May this Thanksgiving be a time to share,
In veneration of God's constant care.

Bess Berry Carr

Harvest Festival

I'm grateful for Thy goodness to provide
The food and daily shelter that I need,
The harvest festival of fruit and grain,
The bounty-reaping from the planted seed;
Dear Lord, I'm thankful for a loving watch
On danger-paths when I am unaware,
For hope that blesses life with guiding light,
For hours of laughter, tears, and wondrous care.

Inez Franck

The Grace of Gratitude

As we receive Thy bounties, Lord,
  Of raiment, shelter, food,
Inspire within our minds and hearts
  The grace of gratitude.

All gifts and blessings that we know
  Come from Thy gracious hand;
Thy overruling love and power
  Encompass sea and land.

The sun that shines, the rains that fall,
  The soft blue sky above,
The winds that blow, the clouds that drift
  Are tokens of Thy love.

The orchards bearing ripened fruit,
  The fields of golden grain,
The trees and flowers everywhere,
  Thy mercies, Lord, contain.

Creator of these lives of ours,
  With every gift endued,
May all our days and years express
  The grace of gratitude.

J. Harold Gwynne, D.D.

On This Day of Thanksgiving

Lansing Christman

Thanksgiving could not have found its way into a more reflective time of year than late November when a season nears its close and the old year itself steps onto the threshold of history. A man is moved to a devout thankfulness.

The farm cellar holds the same good flavors that were so abundant in the garden and field; it holds the same vivid hues and aromas and succulence that were found in the vineyard and orchard. The man harvested, and the woman of the house, looking to everyday needs and to family gatherings, canned berries and fruits and made juices and jellies. Farm vegetables retain much of the flavor and goodness of the seasons. Barrels of apples hold the crispness and the tang of October. Cans of berries hold something of summer, and the delightful flavor of the September vineyard is preserved colorfully in juices, jams, and jellies.

A farm Thanksgiving, when a man's family is around him, is indeed a time of inspiration. It is a good time to reflect on the gathering of crops that is now completed. It is a good time to look to the bounty that this harvest will yield through a season of snow. A man's Thanksgiving may have even deeper significance if he is a fortunate countryman whose ancestral home had been handed down from generation to generation.

A man can be as provident as the hills, and as kind. And on this day, it has long been the family tradition to blend into a dinner of Thanksgiving the goodness and the flavors and the aromas of the year. He can sense the warmth of sunlit fields, the moisture of rain, the tender touch of strawberry leaves against his rugged hands and tanned arms, the rhythmic undulation of timothy as the heavy grass bends in the wind that moves across a meadow in June. He can hear bird songs and woodland streams, the rustling of leaves in a field of corn. Most of all, a countryman says, he has been blessed with the mellowness of maturity in a harvest that now yields its rich and lasting sustenance. He gives devout thanks for the kindness and the wealth of a ripening.

Autumn Gardens

Bitter and fragrant hangs the air
As the days grow short with the season's turning,
And leaves that are filigreed with frost
Smolder and fall with its cold fire burning.

The fragile flowers have burned away;
The warmer flowers now bloom instead.
Delicate pastels give way
To gold and purple and deep-toned red.

Dawn-chill tells of a long cold winter;
Close by the house new wood is stacked.
Languid, the haze drifts over the meadow
As the peace pipes of autumn are slowly smoked.

Julia Collins Ardayne

Our Glorious Gifts

We sing our thanks upon this autumn day
For sunset gleaming through the wine and gold,
For mountains wearing scarves in yellow hues
And harvest pumpkins that the valleys hold.

We heap our baskets now to overflow
With scented apples, nuts, and grapes and pears.
The barns await the farmer's corn and hay;
The wild geese, calling, seek the warm frontiers.

This is a special time within our hearts
To humbly bow and bring our fondest praise,
To let our Father know we reverence Him
For every goodness in our passing days;
Adore the Giver of our glorious gifts,
Remembering the marvels by His hand;
Let golden notes of gladness fill the air
With love to Him who made this fruited land.

Inez Franck

Autumn Colors

Golden leaves are on the ground;
Earth in splendor now is crowned.
Fluttering through the sunlit air
Come the jewels bright and fair,
Garnet-red, a wonder gem,
To crown the Earth's gold diadem.
Green and yellow, russet-brown,
Come more jewels for the crown,
Till in wonderful array,
Earth has reached its crowning day.
Then a magic mantle white
Covers every jewel bright,
Turns them into dullest sod;
But the unseen hand of God
Brings the colors back to Earth
In the day of spring's rebirth,
And the world with glory fills,
In crocus buds and daffodils.

Polly Perkins

In a November Garden

November is the twilight of the year
When nature bids her wildings go to sleep.
I like to slip into my garden now
And pat each little mound that hides a bulb
Which will in spring burst forth in bloom again.
The iris roots lie naked, unafraid
Of winter's chill, but roses must wear wraps
To keep them warm. The somber skies look down,
And silence falls like snow on skittering leaves
That swirl in restless search for winter beds.
It's time for rest and sleep when wild things hear
Their lullaby that's humming in the pines.

Ada Downey Potter

Thanksgiving

The forest is losing its yellow and red.
The corn, in rows in the field, is dead,
Its dry stalks rustle when touched by the breeze;
And the trees are slowly losing their leaves.

The air feels of winter's coming chill;
The grass is brown on meadow and hill;
Trees hang with fruit as red as wine,
And bright color shows through the pumpkin vine.

It's the time of year when our voices we raise
And give our Creator thanksgiving and praise
For all the blessings He's sent our way
All through the year since last Thanksgiving Day.

The harvest is in and the summer's work done.
God's been so good that our cups overrun.
He's given us friends and loved ones galore,
Provided food and shelter and much, much more.

Now as we celebrate this Thanksgiving Day,
We fall on our knees and from our hearts say,
"Thank You, dear Father, in heaven above,
For all of Your blessings, especially Your love."

Cathy Beasley

ideals

Christmas 1982

Gift Catalog

Dear Ideals Friend:

We want to take this opportunity to wish you and yours a blessed Christmas and a most prosperous New Year. Now as in the past we trust you will find the items exhibited in the Ideals catalog a warm and wonderful way to say Merry Christmas to those near and dear. We sincerely appreciate your continued patronage.

Kindest personal regards,

Donald A. Gottschalk

Donald A. Gottschalk
President

❄ C ❄ H ❄ R ❄ I ❄

LET'S CELEBRATE CHRISTMAS is a delightful volume featuring traditions and special holiday celebrations from all over the U.S.A. Perhaps New Mexico's "luminarias" could brighten your family's gathering this year. Or, Christmas customs in Old Sturbridge, Massachusetts might appeal to you. Whatever your choice, this book is sure to become a favorite at Christmas. 80 pages   2-289 $3.95

DECORATING FOR THE HOLIDAYS is indispensible for anyone who wants to create a festive look for their home this season. Expert advice features ideas for advent through twelfth night including wreaths, table pieces and fresh and permanent arrangements. Step-by-step instructions along with color photos of the finished products are included. Make lovely arrangements to keep or to give as gifts. 64 pages   2-286 $2.95

CHRISTMAS AROUND THE WORLD is a colorful collection of unique celebrations and Christmas customs from twenty countries. Featured are France, Germany, England, Poland and Italy to name but a few. For your reading enjoyment or to add a festive flair to family celebrations. 64 pages   2-009 $3.95

FAVORITE CHRISTMAS CAROLS features a popular collection of traditional carols accompanied with delightful artwork. Perfect for carrolling groups this season! 32 pages   8-474 $1.50

THE CHRISTMAS MIRACLE is a heart-warming account of the first Christmas as witnessed by the people at the manger. Interwoven into this narrative are special poems and prose on the true meaning of Christmas. Old master paintings and beautiful contemporary art accompanies the text. 80 pages   2-046 $3.95

HYMNS OF FAITH contains favorite hymns and the story behind their creation. While most of these hymns have been beloved for generations, they will become even more special when you learn how they came into being. 80 pages   2-066 $3.95

Christmas Ideals

CHRISTMAS IDEALS captures the warmth and beauty of this festive holiday season with heart-warming poetry, prose and splendid color photography. Highlighted features include: meditations on a famous Christmas carol in "The Miracle of Silent Night," the cherished legend of St. Nick, and a history of the Christmas creche tradition, featuring lovely Cybis porcelains of "Nicky, the Drummer Boy" and the newly issued "Nativity." Young and old will delight in a Norman Rockwell illustration of Santa, accompanied by the Dr. Donald Stoltz poem, "A Christmas Gift." Share the nearly 40-year-old tradition of this ever-popular issue, and remember to spread some holiday good cheer with a thoughtful gift of Christmas Ideals.

80 pages 1-015 $3.50

SPECIAL 5 copies 7-984 $12.95

SEASON'S GREETINGS is a splendid collection of Christmas verse and photography. It's a colorful way of expressing your thoughts to family and friends this season and it will be treasured always for little more than the cost of a greeting card.

32 pages 2-029 $2.25

CHRISTMAS KITCHEN COOKBOOK contains delicious recipes to make holidays fun and festive! A tempting array of cookies, candies, relishes, jellies and snacks are but a few of the great taste ideas waiting for you!

64 pages 3-635 $3.25

MERRY CHRISTMAS vividly portrays the splendor of this holiday season with prose, poetry and colorful photography. A perfect way to say a special "I'm thinking of you" to friends and relatives!

32 pages 2-459 $2.25

GOURMET CHRISTMAS COOKBOOK offers over 200 delicious recipes for family celebrations and entertaining from appetizers and beverages to quick breads and desserts. The busy cook/hostess will be able to prepare tempting fare with a minimal amount of time and ingredients.

64 pages 3-613 $3.25

CHRISTMAS COOKBOOK features an outstanding collection of traditional holiday menu and gift ideas. These are our readers' favorite recipes, tested by generations. Give your family a special Christmas treat this year and prepare festive holiday fare from this superb volume!

64 pages 3-602 $3.25

CHRISTMAS AROUND THE WORLD COOKBOOK is a selection of menus for festive holiday dining from twenty countries. Choose a complete menu or select courses from different countries to give your Christmas celebration a foreign flair!

64 pages 3-008 $3.25

Four Seasons Gift Set

Celebrate the four seasons with Ideals! This set of four books, THE BEAUTY OF WINTER, THE JOY OF SPRING, THE WARMTH OF SUMMER and THE GIFT OF AUTUMN, beautifully details the special attributes of each season. Join well-known nature writers such as John Burroughs, Walt Whitman, Ralph Waldo Emerson and Henry David Thoreau. Outstanding color photography accompanies the text. A lasting gift to be enjoyed throughout the year.

THE BEAUTY OF WINTER	80 pages	2-073	$4.95
THE JOY OF SPRING	80 pages	2-063	$4.95
THE WARMTH OF SUMMER	80 pages	2-065	$4.95
THE GIFT OF AUTUMN	80 pages	2-072	$4.95
Special . . . Four Seasons Set		7-980	$15.50

G ❄ I ❄ F ❄ T

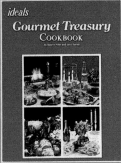

GOURMET TREASURY COOKBOOK is a superb volume containing over 700 delicious recipes for the busy cook and hostess. You'll find dozens of easy, taste-tempting suggestions for appetizers, soups, main dishes, vegetables, quick breads and desserts. Perfect for family meals, entertaining and holiday get-togethers. This is a gift you can be sure will be used again and again! Hardcover.
224 pages 3-024 $9.95

DOWN TO EARTH HOUSEPLANTS is a complete guide to plant care from purchasing healthy plants to decorating ideas. Color photographs and comprehensive descriptions of popular varieties are featured along with charts detailing light conditions, soil and water requirements and transplanting and propagation instructions. A handy reference volume for personal use or as a thoughtful gift.
68 pages 2-387 $2.95

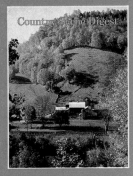

COUNTRY SCENE DIGEST presents the best of country living in this colorful edition. Enjoy recipes featuring down-home goodness, expert gardening tips and new craft ideas complete with step-by-step instructions plus much more! An outstanding value as a gift or for yourself!
224 pages 2-353 $6.95

A TIME FOR LIVING discusses the new life Christ offered to mankind through his death and resurrection. Noted author, Jill Briscoe, shows us how we can live this new life to our fullest ability in the Christian community.
80 pages 2-078 $5.95

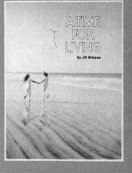

THE BEST OF WEIGHT WATCHERS MAGAZINE features a wealth of information for people who are weight-conscious. Highlights include delicious, low-calorie recipes, step-by-step exercises, fashion and make-up tips, how to keep your spirits up while losing weight and leisure time activities to aid in weight loss.
128 pages 2-621 $4.95

A TIME FOR GIVING discusses the true meaning of this important holiday: how God gave the greatest gift to mankind and how we can incorporate His gift into our own lives at Christmas and all year long. By noted author and lecturer, Jill Briscoe, this volume would be a welcome addition to any home.
80 pages 2-069 $5.95

FAMILY CIRCLE HOLIDAY COOK-BOOK contains year-round holiday menu ideas to delight family and friends. This comprehensive cook-book covers all the major holidays and special occasions with marvelous recipes from casual cookouts to elegant brunches, formal dinners and buffets.
128 pages   9-100 $5.95

THANKSGIVING IDEALS brings you home to celebrate Thanksgiving Day with the poetry, prose and beautiful photography of the autumn season. Enjoy, as the Pilgrims did, the bountiful harvest and many blessings of the land. A lovely painting of the Pilgrims' landing and Thanksgiving prayers and blessings help make this truly a keepsake issue.
80 pages   1-014 $3.50

ALL HOLIDAYS COOKBOOK will help make your entertaining menus varied, attractive and appealing. The recipes in this cookbook range from picnic simplicity to party elegance and cover each major holiday and special occasion throughout the year.
64 pages   3-630 $3.25

VALENTINE IDEALS will warm your heart with the tender sentiments it expresses on this winter holiday. Lovely poetry, prose and photography can help you say "Be My Valentine" and share the special happiness that Valentine's Day can bring.
80 pages   1-016 $3.50

S ❄ H ❄ O ❄ P

PHOTOGRAPHY will give you expert advice on how to make your pictures turn out professionally. Whether you're a beginner or an advanced photographer, this pocket companion will be indispensible!
96 pages   2-900 $2.95

PRESERVING FOOD is a complete guide to preserving fruits and vegetables. Various methods of preserving foods are discussed as well as the necessary preparation, equipment and storage conditions. Enjoy the satisfaction and delicious taste of preserving food!
96 pages   2-905 $2.95

HERBS is a handy reference featuring everything you wanted to know about growing and using herbs. Various types of gardens, medicinal and culinary uses and methods of preserving herbs are discussed.
96 pages   2-903 $2.95

THE IDEAL LIFE: 50 AND OVER is a comprehensive guide for those who wish to start preplanning and enjoying the retirement years. Topics covered include: financial planning, ways to maintain physical and mental health, Medicare, Medicaid, Social Security and second careers.
224 pages   2-081 $5.95

LOOK TO THIS DAY is an inspiring book of verse based on the Sanskrit. The thoughtfully selected poems will be read again and again. Beautiful color photographs complement the text.
80 pages   2-052 $3.95

QUIET REFLECTIONS AND TRANQUIL MOMENTS is a keepsake volume devoted to the poetry of Patience Strong, a favorite of our readers. The selections were personally chosen by the author and an outstanding collection of color photographs illustrate the peace and tranquility found in her writings.
80 pages   2-067 $3.95

COOKIE COOKBOOK features over 200 tasty cookie recipes for sure-to-please family treats and holiday gift-giving. Sixteen color photographs, baking and mailing tips and a list of substitutions accompany the text.
64 pages   3-639 $3.25

NICE AND EASY DESSERTS COOK-BOOK is an outstanding collection of fabulous desserts accompanied by a selection of brilliant color photographs. You're sure to find many delights ranging from crunchy cookies to fabulous tortes!
64 pages   3-612 $3.25

CANDY COOKBOOK contains taste-tempting recipes for all types of candy, including a dietetic section. A comprehensive introduction makes it possible for even the beginner to prepare beautiful gifts this holiday season!
64 pages   3-615 $3.25

CANDY & CANDY MOLDING COOK-BOOK provides easy recipes for making a delicious variety of candy so that even a beginner can produce expert results. A glossary of terms and ingredients is provided as a handy reference.
64 pages   3-015 $3.25

C O O K

MEXICAN COOKBOOK contains recipes gleaned from a diverse and exciting cuisine. Featured is a short history of Mexican cooking, information on the types of ingredients used and a glossary. Chapters range from Antojitos to Postre (Appetizers to Desserts).
64 pages   3-000 $3.25

LOW CALORIE COOKBOOK incorporates tips of how to cut calories in everyday cooking while highlighting flavor and eye appeal in dishes the whole family will enjoy. Each recipe gives the calorie content per serving. Features recipes such as Rock Lobster Continental, Veal Scallopini with Mushrooms and Blueberry-Banana Bread.
64 pages   3-003 $3.25

SOUP, SALAD, SANDWICH COOK-BOOK has over 200 tempting recipes for what usually is thought to be ordinary fare. This delightful collection is accompanied with brilliant color photographs and serving suggestions.
64 pages   3-001 $3.25

COOKING FOR TWO COOKBOOK is designed to meet the needs of those who are buying and preparing foods for just two people. The amount of protein, fat and carbohydrate for each recipe is given. Included are superb selections such as Turbot de Joie, Italian Quiche and Bacon Crescent Rolls.
64 pages   3-004 $3.25

CHINESE COOKBOOK is an introduction to Chinese cooking that makes learning fun as well as easy. Included are methods of cooking, a glossary of common terms, an introduction to basic cutting methods and types of cuisine such as Szechuan and Cantonese.
64 pages   3-002 $3.25

GROUND MEAT COOKBOOK will show you how to use your culinary talents to make delicious fare out of various types of ground meat. These taste-tempting recipes use a cut of meat to full advantage and are easy on the budget.
64 pages   3-005 $3.25

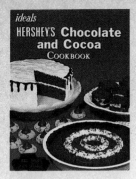

HERSHEY'S CHOCOLATE AND COCOA COOKBOOK is a superb collection of recipes ranging from delicious cookies and candies to mouth-watering pies and tortes. Enjoy such luscious treats as Butter Almond Crunch, Chocolate Strawberry Bombe and Cocoa Chiffon-Cloud Pie.
64 pages   3-007 $3.25

PIES AND PASTRIES COOKBOOK contains fabulous recipes for a wide variety of exquisite pies and pastries. Also included are basic instructions for making different pie shells, crumb crusts, latticework tops and perfect meringues.
64 pages   3-011 $3.25

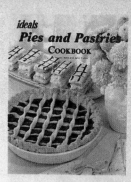

EASY APPETIZER COOKBOOKS is a superb collection of easy, delicious recipes for hot and cold appetizers to tempt both the cook and her guests. Perfect for year-round entertaining as well as festive holiday occasions. Beautiful color photographs illustrate the chapters.
64 pages   3-618 $3.25

EASY CAKE DECORATING provides easy-to-understand instructions for designing beautifully decorated cakes. Beginners can learn professional techniques in sixteen basic lessons. Many illustrations are provided.
64 pages   3-622 $3.25

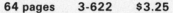

B O O K S

THE DANNON YOGURT COOKBOOK includes many fabulous recipes from appetizers to desserts, using plain yogurt and many of the luscious flavors that Dannon offers. Low-fat yogurt is a perfect substitute for buttermilk, sour cream and mayonnaise in many dishes and can contribute to good health and nutrition.
64 pages   3-010 $3.25

GOURMET ON THE GO COOKBOOK is a superb collection of easy-to-prepare, delicious recipes for the busy cook during the holidays and all year round! Beautiful color photographs will give you many serving ideas.
64 pages   3-631 $3.25

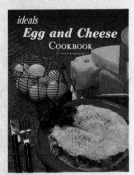

EGG AND CHEESE COOKBOOK features unique recipes from breakfast to desserts using nutritious, versatile and economical eggs and cheese. Try such tasty fare as Cheesy Puffs, Broccoli-Chicken Quiche and Golden Stuffed Pork Chops.
64 pages   3-009 $3.25

HOLIDAY COOKING FOR KIDS provides recipes for holiday meals from appetizers to desserts that children can prepare themselves. Safety instructions are also provided, along with a list of equipment needed, ingredients and step-by-step instructions for each recipe.
48 pages   3-014 $3.25

FOOD PROCESSOR COOKBOOK features over 200 tempting recipes. There is an introduction to the basic techniques of cutting, including a description of various blades and their functions and necessary safety precautions. A list of food equivalents, the amount of unprocessed food needed to yield a certain processed quantity, is also included.
64 pages   3-006 $3.25

I CAN COOK COOKBOOK contains delicious recipes for the junior chef that the whole family will enjoy. Safety precautions plus step-by-step instructions ensure success for the beginning cook.
48 pages   8-935 $2.95

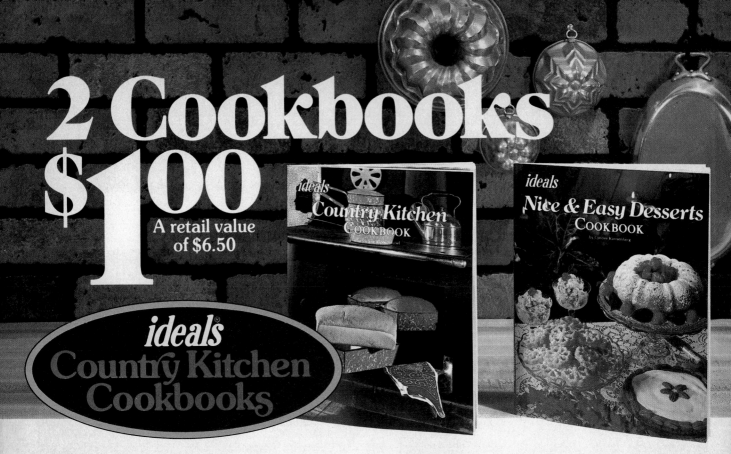

IDEALS' BINDER
BEAUTIFUL BINDER HOLDS 8 ISSUES OF IDEALS!

An Ideals' binder is a must for anyone who treasures the lasting beauty of Ideals. Our colorful cover design features the four seasons captured in brilliant photography on a deluxe vinyl exterior. Metal rod binding eliminates any unsightly hole punching. Sturdy construction protects your issues and prevents damage. Perfect for your own collection or as a gift to the special person you give an Ideals subscription to.
10-713 $5.95

IDEALS' COOKBOOK VIEWER
CONVENIENT LUCITE VIEWER PROTECTS BOOKS!

Our handy cookbook viewer is made of strong, durable lucite. It gives you a clear view of the cookbook page you are using while holding the book firmly in place. Smudges and spatters wipe clean. The viewer folds flat for storage. It may also be used for the home repairman, craftsman or student. A unique gift to be used year round.
10-716 $6.95

How To Order . . .

BY MAIL

1. Enter your complete name and address (including zip code) in the area provided in the upper left hand corner of the order blank.

2. Enter QUANTITY to be ordered for each item in the appropriate column under quantity.

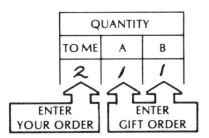

For your personal order enter quantity in column "To Me." All items entered in columns "A" or "B" will be sent as gifts from you to the persons indicated in the corresponding gift address areas.

3. Enter AMOUNT (quantity x price) in the box provided for each item.

4. Total your complete catalogue order (including gift shipments) and enter in SUB TOTAL.

5. Add SUB TOTAL and POSTAGE and enter in TOTAL. Add tax if applicable.

6. Add SUBSCRIPTIONS enrolled on the special card in the catalog. If your GRAND TOTAL is $20.00 or more you may choose a FREE GIFT! See other side for details.

7. For your catalogue purchase indicate your choice of payment plans. If you are using your credit card, be sure to include your signature, expiration date and your complete account number. Separate the order form from the envelope, fold your order form, enclose your check or money order and your subscription card in the envelope and mail.

BY TELEPHONE

CALL TOLL FREE
1-800-558-4343

Wisconsin Residents
Call Collect (414) 771-2700

Ideals will be pleased to take your order by phone. Our telephone department is open Monday thru Friday, 8 AM to 4:30 PM (C.S.T.). For questions or product information, please call our regular office number, (414) 771-2774

Thank you.

ideals PUBLISHING CORPORATION
P.O. BOX 2100
MILWAUKEE, WI 53201

D701

MY ADDRESS

YOUR NAME _____

ADDRESS_____

CITY _____

STATE _____ ZIP _____

TELEPHONE NO. _____

Remit in U.S. Currency

☐ **Payment Enclosed**

☐ **Bill Me**

☐ Charge my **Master Charge**

☐ Charge my **BankAmericard/VISA**   Exp. Date

Acct. No. ☐☐☐☐☐☐☐☐☐☐☐☐☐ ☐☐☐☐

SIGNATURE _____

FOR GIFT ORDERS:
- Fill in above section
- Fill in quantity A on order blank for 1st Gift Address; and quantity B for 2nd Gift Address.
- If additional gifts are to be ordered, write instructions on a plain sheet and enclose with your order.

GIFT ADDRESS A

Please send the items I have indicated to be shipped to ADDRESS A as gifts from me to my friend listed below:

GIFT NAME _____

ADDRESS _____

CITY _____

STATE _____ ZIP _____

GIFT ADDRESS B

Please send the items I have indicated to be shipped to ADDRESS B as gifts from me to my friend listed below:

GIFT NAME _____

ADDRESS _____

CITY _____

STATE _____ ZIP _____

ORDERING INSTRUCTIONS

	QUANTITY	
TO ME	A	B
2	1	1
ENTER YOUR ORDER	ENTER GIFT ORDER	

- Enter quantity to be ordered
- Enter your order
- Enter gift orders
- Enter amount (quantity x price) in box provided for each item.
- Total your order as indicated.
- To expedite your order, use our Toll Free Service 1-800-558-4343 WI. Residents Call Collect (414) 771-2700

CODE	TITLE	QUANTITY ME	A	B	PRICE	AMOUNT
	CHRISTMAS					
2-289	Let's Celebrate Christmas				$3.95	
2-009	Christmas Around/World				$3.95	
2-046	The Christmas Miracle				$3.95	
2-286	Decorating For/Holidays				$2.95	
8-474	Favorite Christmas Carols				$1.50	
2-066	Hymns of Faith				$3.95	
7-984	Special—5 Christmas Ideals A $17.50 Value				$12.95 per 5	
1-015	1982 Christmas Ideals				$3.50	
2-029	Season's Greetings				$2.25	
2-459	Merry Christmas				$2.25	
3-602	Christmas Cookbook				$3.25	
3-635	Christmas Kitchen Ckbk				$3.25	
3-613	Gourmet Christmas Ckbk				$3.25	
3-008	Xmas Around/World Ckbk				$3.25	
	GIFT SHOP					
7-980	Special—4 Seasons Set A $19.80 Value				$15.50 per set	
2-073	The Beauty of Winter				$4.95	
2-063	The Joy of Spring				$4.95	
2-065	The Warmth of Summer				$4.95	
2-072	The Gift of Autumn				$4.95	
3-024	Gourmet Treasury Ckbk				$9.95	
2-353	Country Scene Digest				$6.95	
2-621	Best of Weight Watchers				$4.95	
2-387	Down to Earth Houseplants				$2.95	
2-078	A Time For Living				$5.95	
2-069	A Time For Giving				$5.95	
9-100	Family Circle Holiday Ckbk				$5.95	
3-630	All Holiday Cookbook				$3.25	
1-014	1982 Thanksgiving Ideals				$3.50	
1-016	1983 Valentine Ideals				$3.50	
2-900	Photography				$2.95	
2-903	Herbs				$2.95	
2-052	Look To This Day				$3.95	
2-905	Preserving Food				$2.95	
2-081	Ideal Life: 50 And Over				$5.95	
2-067	Quiet Reflections/Moments				$3.95	
	COOKBOOK					
3-639	Cookie				$3.25	
3-615	Candy				$3.25	
3-612	Nice & Easy Desserts				$3.25	
3-015	Candy & Candy Molding				$3.25	
3-000	Mexican				$3.25	
3-001	Soup, Salad, Sandwich				$3.25	
3-002	Chinese				$3.25	
3-003	Low Calorie				$3.25	
3-004	Cooking For Two				$3.25	
3-005	Ground Meat				$3.25	
3-007	Hershey's Chocolate/Cocoa				$3.25	
3-618	Easy Appetizer				$3.25	
3-011	Pies and Pastry				$3.25	
3-622	Cake Decorating				$3.25	
3-010	Yogurt				$3.25	
3-009	Egg And Cheese				$3.25	
3-006	Food Processor				$3.25	
3-631	Gourmet On The Go				$3.25	
3-014	Holiday Cooking For Kids				$3.25	
8-935	I Can Cook				$3.25	
	MISCELLANEOUS					
10-713	Ideals Binder				$5.95	
10-716	Cookbook Viewer				$6.95	

HOW MUCH DOES $1.00 BUY TODAY?

At the service station, barely enough to get your car home—at the grocery store, hardly enough to put in a bag. That's what makes this SPECIAL $1.00 OFFER from Ideals so exciting!

Just complete the order card (attached) and send it with $1.00 for your introduction to the IDEALS COUNTRY KITCHEN PLAN. We'll rush you 2 regular editions of Ideals Cookbooks (Nice and Easy Desserts and Country Kitchen) and a FREE BONUS recipe card collection . . . . . a $7.50 retail value . . . . . all for just $1.00!

● NO HIDDEN CHARGES ● NO CLUB TO JOIN ● CANCEL ANYTIME ●
● NO POSTAGE & HANDLING FEES ● NO SALES TAX ●

After receiving your introductory shipment, you will receive 2 new cookbooks each month for the next 3 months . . . and you pay only $5.50 for each shipment!

The 5th shipment will complete your collection. You can pay for these 18 cookbooks in the month received and earn a SPECIAL DISCOUNT . . . or simply pay $5.50 that month and $5.50 per month for the next 8 months. Many of our readers call this the "pay as you cook plan." But there is more . . . with the 5th shipment, we will send you a handsome LUCITE COOKBOOK VIEWER (a $6.95 value) . . . ABSOLUTELY FREE!

The 26 books in this collection are listed on the following page. Perhaps you may see some books that you've already purchased. If that is the case, you know how great they are. Others participating in this plan who have found similar "duplicates" use these additional copies as wonderful gifts. Remember each book costs you $2.75 or less!

START YOUR COLLECTION TODAY!

● You can mail your card and payment in the envelope with your catalog order—but this offer does not apply toward the FREE GIFT offer for catalog purchases.

● Sorry, but we cannot process gift orders—the collection must be sent to the same address that will pay for the shipment.

● Fill out the card and place it along with $1.00 in an envelope TODAY! (We recommend a check or money order.)

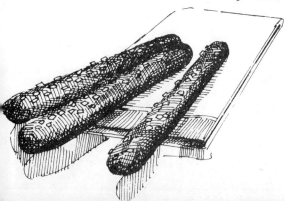

CODE	TITLE	QUANTITY			PRICE	AMOUNT
	HOME IMPROVEMENT	ME	A	B		
6-119	Children's Rooms/Play Areas				$3.95	
6-125	Home Appliance Repairs				$3.95	
6-124	Guide to Wood Refinishing				$3.95	
6-123	Wallcover/Panel/Paint/Paper				$3.95	
6-105	Guide To Fireplaces				$3.95	
6-107	Guide To Roofing And Siding				$3.95	
6-120	Guide To Fastening				$3.95	
6-116	Guide To Swimming Pools				$3.95	
6-114	Vacation Homes				$3.95	
6-117	Guide To Landscaping				$3.95	
6-112	Build Your Own Home				$9.95	
6-111	Additional Rooms				$3.95	
6-101	Guide To Tools				$3.95	
6-113	Home Additions				$3.95	
6-110	Finding/Fixing Older Home				$3.95	
6-100	Money Saving Home Repair				$3.95	
6-104	Shelves And Built-Ins				$3.95	
6-103	Kitchen Planning				$3.95	
6-109	Home Plans For The 80's				$3.95	
6-102	Bathroom Planning				$3.95	
	CHILDREN					
8-923	The Littlest Angel				$3.25	
8-010	Thingumajig/Manners				$3.25	
8-024	Christmas Comes To/Mountain				$3.25	
8-942	Bear/Slept Through Christmas				$3.25	
8-031	Thingumajig/Health & Safety				$3.25	
8-041	Rikki-Tikki-Tavi				$3.25	
8-042	The White Seal				$3.25	
8-933	Little Sleepyheads				$1.95	
8-008	I'm Thankful Each Day				$2.50	
8-006	That's What A Friend Is				$2.50	
8-017	Bible Stories				$3.25	
8-009	When Jesus Was A Little Boy				$3.25	
8-023	Prayers For Children				$3.25	
8-038	Christian Nursery Rhymes				$3.25	
8-022	Common Senses				$4.95	
8-940	Ideals For Kids				$3.95	
8-043	Twelve Days of Christmas				$3.25	
8-015	Nedobeck's Numbers				$3.25	
8-016	Nedobeck's Alphabet				$3.25	
8-924	Big Blue Marble Atlas				$9.95	
7-903	Special—4 Farfetched Pets A $7.80 Value				$6.25 per 4	
8-027	Your Pet Bear				$1.95	
8-028	Your Pet Gorilla				$1.95	
8-029	Your Pet Elephant				$1.95	
8-030	Your Pet Kangaroo				$1.95	
8-249	The Tooth Chicken				$1.25	
7-986	Special—5 Book Set—1 Each Titles Listed—A $13.40 Value				$10.95 per 5	
8-262	Dicken's Christmas Carol				$2.95	
8-498	Night Before Christmas				$2.50	
8-454	The Story of Christmas				$2.50	
8-514	Amanda's Tree				$2.95	
8-448	Jolly Old Santa Claus				$2.50	
7-904	Special—6 Book Zoo Collection A $7.50 Value				$5.95 per 6	
7-967	Offer A—6 Good Friends A $7.50 Value				$5.95 per 6	
7-964	Offer B—6 Good Friends A $7.50 Value				$5.95 per 6	
7-905	Offer C—6 Good Friends A $7.50 Value				$5.95 per 6	

CODE	TITLE	QUANTITY			PRICE	AMOUN
	GREETINGS	ME	A	B		
7-977	Special—12 Christmas Greetings—A $12.00 Value				$9.95 per 12	
5-819	Christmas Greetings				$1.00	
7-978	Special—12 Christmas Blessings—A $12.00 Value				$9.95 per 12	
5-820	Christmas Blessings				$1.00	
7-979	Special—12 Pack—6 Each Greetings & Blessings				$9.95 per 12	
7-973	Special—Variety Pack 1 Each Of 12 Titles				$9.95 per pk.	
5-826	To Comfort You				$1.00	
5-812	A Special Thank You				$1.00	
5-774	From This Day Forward				$1.00	
5-806	God's Orchard				$1.00	
5-776	On Your Graduation Day				$1.00	
5-816	Get Well Soon				$1.00	
5-815	On Your Birthday				$1.00	
5-779	Remembering/Anniversary				$1.00	
5-809	To The Bride And Groom				$1.00	
5-777	You Are My Friend				$1.00	
5-808	Happy Birthday				$1.00	
5-772	To The Happy Parents				$1.00	

PLEASE TOTAL YOUR ORDER

SUB TOTAL BOOKS $ _____

ADD $1.75 FOR EACH ADDRESS SHIPPED $ _____

TOTAL $ _____

WI RESIDENTS ADD 5% SALES TAX $ _____

SUBSCRIPTIONS $ _____

Free Gift if $20 or more! **GRAND TOTAL** $ _____

If **GRAND TOTAL** is for $20.00 or more, choose EITHER Free Gift below:

CREATING DESIGNS WITH DRIED FLOWERS will give you new, interesting ideas on how to add a decorative flair to your home. Noted author Harold Cook describes techniques for preserving, drying and arranging flowers, leaves and seed heads.
64 pages   2-288   ☐ FREE GIFT

LET'S WRAP IT UP! will show you how to gift wrap beautifully with a few basic ideas, some inexpensive materials and a little imagination. There are unique gift wrapping ideas for many occasions and holiday celebrations throughout the year.
64 pages   2-861   ☐ FREE GIFT

Do You Have
A Special Friend
Who Would Enjoy Receiving
A FREE Ideals Catalog?

Simply fill in the complete names, and addresses of those special friends who would like to receive a FREE Ideals catalog.

Please Send a FREE Ideals Catalog to:

NAME _____

ADDRESS _____

CITY_____

STATE _____ZIP _____

NAME _____

ADDRESS _____

CITY_____

STATE _____ZIP _____

Moisten here.

Fold along perforation and tear. **Before Sealing — IS YOUR CHECK OR MONEY ORDER SIGNED PROPERLY?**

**Remove This Section
Before Mailing**

ideals
PUBLISHING CORPORATION
P.O. BOX 2100
MILWAUKEE, WISCONSIN 53201

PLACE
STAMP
HERE

Give the Beauty of Ideals
Year-round to Yourself or a Friend
... and Save Up to 50%

Something wonderful for everyone in the family.

IDEALS celebrates the things we cherish most

The beauty of our country ... from the craggy coast of Maine to the wave-kissed shores of Hawaii ... from the mansions of the South to the mountains of the Northwest ... the natural and man-made wonders of our nation are brought to life in vivid full color in IDEALS. (A gift subscription to IDEALS is like a scenic excursion ticket to the beauty spots of America!)

Family life ... and the occasions that bring us closer together are celebrated in IDEALS: a parent's love ... the joys of childhood ... the family fun of making ice cream ~~~~ing a Jack-O-Lantern ... and all the other ~~~~nts that enrich our lives.

~~~~ the colorful local customs ... you'll find ~~~~ to be

EACH NEW ISSUE FEATU~~~~

- 80 advertising-free pages of exquisite qu~~~~
- Full-color photographs of nature, peopl~~~~ interiors, crafts and antiques.
- Prose and photography combined to ~~~~ informative articles.
- Poetry and fascinating short stories.
- Art reproductions to frame.

Save 43% • 8 issues ~~~~
a $28.00 value — *Only $15.95*

Save 50% • 16 issues (2 years)
a $56.00 value — *Only $27.95*

Foreign & Canadian subscriptions
add $4.00 per year for postage

Use the attached order form for
your personal and gift subscriptions.

(co~~~~

Gifts—rememb~~~~
in your life with an uplifting g~~~~
subscription.

Subscriptions—give a gift of
beauty to yourself and to your family.

CHILDREN'S ROOMS & PLAY AREAS shows how to design and execute beautiful, functional rooms to help children learn creatively. Projects include bedrooms, attics, play yards and tree houses.
96 pages   6-119 $3.95

HOMEOWNER'S GUIDE TO WOOD REFINISHING explains everything the homeowner needs to know to finish or refinish any type of wood. Step-by-step instructions include stripping, sanding, finishing, antiquing, staining and varnishing.
96 pages   6-124 $3.95

HOME APPLIANCE REPAIR GUIDE explains the techniques and tool requirements necessary for the homeowner's basic repair of common large and small household appliances.
96 pages   6-125 $3.95

WALLCOVERINGS: PANELING, PAINTING & PAPERING details instructions and diagrams for installing wood paneling, painting walls and wallpapering. Instructions for stucco and special finishes are also included.
96 pages   6-123 $3.95

H O M E   I M P

HOMEOWNER'S GUIDE TO FIRE-PLACES is a comprehensive guide to building attractive, efficient fireplaces and wood-burning stoves. Many detailed diagrams are included.
96 pages   6-105 $3.95

HOMEOWNER'S GUIDE TO SWIM-MING POOLS is a complete reference to buying, building and maintaining a swimming pool. Topics include site selection, style and maintenance.
96 pages   6-116 $3.95

HOMEOWNER'S GUIDE TO ROOF-ING AND SIDING encompasses renovating and modernizing the exterior of your home by reroofing and residing. Alternative ways of contracting the projects are examined.
96 pages   6-107 $3.95

PLANNING AND BUILDING VA-CATION HOMES details plans for constructing various types of vacation homes without the aid of a contractor. Includes a wide range of designs.
96 pages   6-114 $3.95

HOMEOWNER'S GUIDE TO FAS-TENING ANYTHING is a complete volume illustrating fastening methods, their various uses and how they function.
96 pages   6-120 $3.95

HOMEOWNER'S GUIDE TO LAND-SCAPING is a well-illustrated guide to landscape design and techniques to aid homeowners in achieving a professional look.
96 pages   6-117 $3.95

HOW TO BUILD YOUR OWN HOME encompasses every facet of home construction. In 50 detailed chapters, the homeowner will find information from financing and choosing a site to finishing the driveway and landscaping. Over 600 photographs, drawings, charts and diagrams accompany the text.
352 pages   6-112 $9.95

HOMEOWNER'S TOOLS offers information on everything you need to know about tools: how to choose them, use them, when and where to rent, buy or borrow, safety precautions and maintenance.
96 pages   6-101 $3.95

FINISHING OFF ADDITIONAL ROOMS is a comprehensive homeowner's guide to finishing off unused rooms, basements and attics for additional living space. A beautiful full-color section illustrates how to plan and design efficient use of space.
96 pages   6-111 $3.95

PLANNING AND BUILDING HOME ADDITIONS is a complete manual to aid homeowners who want to increase living space from a simple garage conversion to a major second-story addition.
96 pages   6-113 $3.95

ROVEMENT

FINDING AND FIXING THE OLDER HOME contains guidelines on what to look for in an older home, such as structural and cosmetic strengths and weaknesses and how much time and money should be invested over and above the purchase price to bring the dwelling up to current standards. Basic instructions for repairing and remodeling both the interior and exterior are included.
96 pages   6-110 $3.95

KITCHEN PLANNING AND REMODELING offers a comprehensive selection of ideas for helping the homeowner modernize the kitchen to be efficient and workable. The easy-to-follow instructions cover all aspects of kitchen improvement: planning and design, color use, lighting, ventilation, counters and sinks, cabinets and space-saving ideas and energy-saving devices.
96 pages   6-109 $3.95

MONEY SAVING HOME REPAIR GUIDE features detailed instructions and diagrams to enable the average homeowner, with little or no experience, to handle almost any repair without the services of a contractor. Homeowners will be able to repair squeaking and sagging floors, cracked walls and ceilings, damaged roofs, windows and doors. Also basic electrical and plumbing problems.
96 pages   6-100 $3.95

HOME PLANS FOR THE 80'S contains designs for 188 homes, featuring exterior renderings and complete floor plans. Types of plans presented include: Tudor, Early Colonial, French, Spanish and Contemporary. Special sections include: vacation homes and low/medium cost homes. Sources for the specific plans are listed.
96 pages   6-109 $3.95

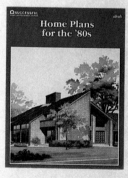

SHELVES AND BUILT-INS is the answer for the homeowner at wits' end for lack of ample storage space. It provides step-by-step instructions and construction details for building shelves, counters, cabinets, bookcases and storage units. Information on how to work with various materials is provided along with specific projects such as kitchen cabinets, bathroom vanities, and closets.
96 pages   6-104 $3.95

BATHROOM PLANNING AND REMODELING contains easy-to-follow instructions enabling the homeowner to undertake bathroom remodeling with ease and confidence. Whether you are planning and designing a new bathroom or improving and remodeling an existing one, you will find a wealth of ideas among the beautiful contemporary and traditional plans and styles in this volume.
96 pages   6-102 $3.95

THE LITTLEST ANGEL is the delightful story of a small cherub who turns heaven upside down but who gives a special meaning to giving as he presents his most cherished possession to God's new Son. An enduring favorite. Hardcover.
32 pages   8-923 $3.25

CHRISTMAS COMES TO MONSTER MOUNTAIN features a popular Ideals' character, Ted E. Bear, narrating the story of how the world's most feared monsters find the warmth and spirit of Christmas. Accompanied by brilliant, full-color artwork by noted artist, Rick Reinert. Hardcover.
32 pages   8-024 $3.25

THINGUMAJIG BOOK OF MANNERS shows children fascinating creatures who behave disgracefully in public and in their own company! The scenes are accompanied with captions featuring the proper behavior in each situation. This book of un-manners is guaranteed to keep children away from bad habits! Hardcover.
32 pages   8-010 $3.25

THE BEAR WHO SLEPT THROUGH CHRISTMAS features the popular television hero, Ted E. Bear, who longs to celebrate Christmas in a special way. This heart-warming story will appeal to parents and children alike! Watch for Ted E. Bear on TV this season! Hardcover.
32 pages   8-942 $3.25

❄ C ❄ H ❄ I ❄ L

THE THINGUMAJIG BOOK OF HEALTH AND SAFETY is designed to show children the value in following health and safety rules. Unique illustrations accompany the delightful verse and make learning a fun experience for both parents and children.
32 pages   8-031 $3.25

LITTLE SLEEPYHEADS is a beautiful collection of favorite bedtime stories lovingly illustrated by Frances Hook. Enjoy such classics as "In the Land of Counterpane," "There Once Was a Puffin" and "One, Two, Buckle My Shoe."
32 pages   8-933 $1.95

RIKKI-TIKKI-TAVI—In this Kipling classic, Chuck Jones has captivated TV audiences with his delightful illustrations of a lovable little mongoose named Rikki-tikki-tavi.
48 pages   8-041 $4.95

I'M THANKFUL EACH DAY portrays a child's heart-warmingly simple expression of gratitude for everything from apples to sunshine. Clever, full-color art accompanies the verse.
24 pages   8-008 $2.50

THE WHITE SEAL is the timeless tale by Rudyard Kipling that recounts a rare white seal's growth into maturity, as featured on TV by artist Chuck Jones.
48 pages   8-042 $4.95

THAT'S WHAT A FRIEND IS describes for children the many facets of a close friendship . . . from bad times to good times. Accompanied by charming, color artwork.
32 pages   8-006 $2.50

BIBLE STORIES FOR CHILDREN brings the characters of the New Testament to life adding yet another dimension to children's most beloved Bible parables. Enchanting full-color art. Hardcover.
32 pages   8-017 $3.25

PRAYERS FOR CHILDREN captures the unique charm of favorite children's prayers. Whether before dinner or before bedtime, children will delight in repeating the classic verses. Features beautiful color artwork. Hardcover.
32 pages   8-023 $3.25

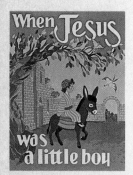

WHEN JESUS WAS A LITTLE BOY focuses on the childhood of Jesus. Children can readily identify with the little boy who does many of the same things they do in daily life. Lovely color art accompanies the verses.
32 pages   8-009 $2.50

CHRISTIAN NURSERY RHYMES is a richly illustrated volume that subtly teaches Christian values through favorite nursery rhymes.
48 pages   8-038 $4.95

COMMON SENSES is a beautifully illustrated collection of stories featuring five delightful animal characters who demonstrate just how important each of our five senses is. Rick Reinert's art brings the stories to life. Hardcover.
48 pages   8-022 $4.95

NEDOBECK'S NUMBERS BOOK makes learning numbers a thoroughly enjoyable experience for both youngsters and parents. Lovable, full color animal characters illustrate the verses. Hardcover.
32 pages   8-015 $3.25

IDEALS FOR KIDS is a special collection of favorite children's stories, poems and games. Brilliant color photography and artwork are sure to delight youngsters of all ages. It need not be a rainy day for children to find this volume entertaining!
64 pages   9-40 $3.95

NEDOBECK'S ALPHABET BOOK parades the fascinating characters of Don Nedobeck through the ABC's and gives letter learning a whole new appeal for both youngsters and parents. Full-color illustrations. Hardcover.
32 pages   8-016 $3.25

NEDOBECK'S TWELVE DAYS OF CHRISTMAS is a highly imaginative version of the traditional Christmas carol. Don Nedobeck combines wry humor with the whimsical characters of his illustrations, establishing a unique theme of friendship.
32 pages   8-043 $3.25

BIG BLUE MARBLE ATLAS is based on the popular television series for children. This colorful, deluxe edition is more than just a collection of maps: children learn of the culture and economic environment of the world's nations as well as their geography. Hardcover.
168 pages   8-924 $9.95

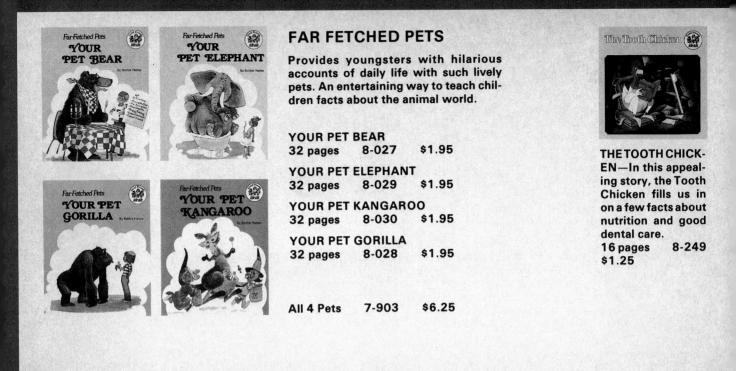

FAR FETCHED PETS

Provides youngsters with hilarious accounts of daily life with such lively pets. An entertaining way to teach children facts about the animal world.

YOUR PET BEAR
32 pages   8-027 $1.95

YOUR PET ELEPHANT
32 pages   8-029 $1.95

YOUR PET KANGAROO
32 pages   8-030 $1.95

YOUR PET GORILLA
32 pages   8-028 $1.95

All 4 Pets   7-903 $6.25

THE TOOTH CHICK-
EN—In this appeal-
ing story, the Tooth
Chicken fills us in
on a few facts about
nutrition and good
dental care.
16 pages   8-249
$1.25

C H I L

Special . . . a $13.40 value!
5 book set   7-986 $10.95

DICKENS' CHRISTMAS
CAROL
THE NIGHT BEFORE
CHRISTMAS
STORY OF CHRISTMAS
FOR CHILDREN
AMANDA'S TREE
JOLLY OLD SANTA CLAUS

THE STORY OF CHRISTMAS FOR CHILDREN tells the Nativity story in rhyming verse. Children can easily understand the special meaning of this important holiday. Beautiful artwork accompanies the text.
32 pages   8-454 $2.50

DICKENS' CHRISTMAS CAROL tells the ageless story of the true meaning of Christmas giving. Tiny Tim, Scrooge and the ghosts of Christmas come alive in beautiful color artwork. Make this story a holiday tradition for someone you love!
48 pages   8-262 $2.95

AMANDA'S TREE is a story of love and giving at Christmas time. A small girl shares a very special Christmas tree with those in need of cheer and finds that perhaps sharing is the best Christmas gift of all!
32 pages   8-514 $2.95

THE NIGHT BEFORE CHRISTMAS portrays Clement Moore's famous poem in beautiful full-color illustrations. Adults and children will both enjoy this delightful holiday tale!
32 pages   8-498 $2.50

JOLLY OLD SANTA CLAUS tells of the joyous activity at the North Pole as Santa and his elves prepare for the busiest night of the year . . . Christmas Eve! George Hinke's superb artwork complements the story.
32 pages   8-448 $2.50

ZOO BABIES COLLECTION

A $7.50 Value Only $5.95

Through captivating color photography the babies of the San Diego Zoo and Wild Animal Park are showcased in charming stories designed for early readers. These books offer children a unique balance of fact with fiction as the animals relate their own stories.

Alberta
the Gorilla

Nanuck
the Polar Bear

Sydney
the Koala

Sasha
the Cheetah

Wilbur and Orville
the Otter Twins

Zelda
the Zebra

All 6 Zoo Babies   7-904 $5.95

D ❄ R ❄ E ❄ N ❄

3 GOOD FRIENDS ASSORTMENTS   Each A $7.50 Value Only $5.95

These humorous stories will delight children of all ages. Each book contains 16 colorful pages.

Dugan
the Duck

Gloomy Gus
the Hippopotamus

Freddie
the Frog

Ulysses S. Ant
and Robert E. Flea

Emil
the Eagle

Elihu
the Elephant

OFFER A — All 6 books above   7-967 $5.95

Bingo
the Bear

Woolly
the Wolf

Isadore
the Dinosaur

Toulouse
the Moose

Earl
the Squirrel

Spunky
the Monkey

OFFER B — All 6 books above   7-964 $5.95

Tuffy
the Tiger

Morgan
the Mule

Henry
the Hound

Melissa
the Mouse

Kenny
the Kitty

Ringo
the Raccoon

OFFER C — All 6 books above   7-905 $5.95

CHRISTMAS GREETINGS will say so much more than just a greeting card! Let this delightful booklet express your holiday sentiments for you! A fine selection of seasonal verse is accompanied by brilliant color photography. Receive extra savings when you purchase sets of twelve! Complete with envelopes.

5-819 $1.00
Special . . . set of 12   7-977 $9.95

CHRISTMAS BLESSINGS will convey the special meaning of the most important Christian holiday in joyous verse. Beautiful photography complements biblical passages and heartfelt poetry. Special savings are offered on sets of twelve! Complete with envelopes.

5-820 $1.00
Special . . . set of 12   7-978 $9.95

Special set of 6 Greetings
and 6 Blessings   7-979 $9.95

ideals
PUBLISHING CORPORATION
11315 WATERTOWN PLANK RD.
MILWAUKEE, WISCONSIN 53226

GREETINGS

All Occasion Booklets

This selection of all occasion greeting booklets will serve every need you have for greeting cards and yet say so much more! Each one has a special theme, beautifully expressed in thoughtful verse and brilliant color photography and will be a lasting remembrance for the special people in your life! As a set, these twelve greeting booklets are an outstanding value! Complete with envelopes.

TO COMFORT YOU	5-825	$1.00
A SPECIAL THANK YOU	5-812	$1.00
FROM THIS DAY FORWARD	5-774	$1.00
GOD'S ORCHARD	5-806	$1.00
GRADUATION DAY	5-776	$1.00
GET WELL SOON	5-816	$1.00
ON YOUR BIRTHDAY	5-815	$1.00
REMEMBERING YOUR ANNIVERSARY	5-779	$1.00
TO THE BRIDE AND GROOM	5-809	$1.00
YOU ARE MY FRIEND	5-777	$1.00
HAPPY BIRTHDAY	5-808	$1.00
TO THE HAPPY PARENTS	5-772	$1.00
Special . . . set of all 12	7-973	$9.95

It's the Season

I can smell the roasting turkey;
I can smell the mincemeat pie.
I can almost taste the goodies
On the table, me, oh my!
There's a certain something lurking;
There's a din that fills the air
With the glow of happy faces
That are beaming everywhere.
It is much too cold and snowy
On the outside looking in,
And the fireside chair is waiting
For the stories to begin.
We have gathered all the firewood
That will warm us, there's no doubt,
As we make ourselves so cozy
On the inside looking out.
The excitement now is mounting;
No one needs to say a thing,
For the atmosphere has told me
It is now the time to sing.
Yes, we'll sing about the good times,
Even sing about the bad.
We will thank the Lord for all things
That He gave us and be glad.
For it is the gayest season;
The nostalgia's really great;
It makes my insides tingle
Just to know we'll celebrate.
I would like to share my feelings;
Here's my message loud and clear:
May the good Lord bless and keep you;
Hope you have a happy year.

Dottie Carriedo

A Thankful Heart

May we always each remember
   On this special day
Many blessings that are ours
   All along the way.

May we with deep humility
   Forever have a part
In expressing gratitude
   From a thankful heart.

Grant us strength to do our best
   In each daily task;
To be worthy of this day
   We would humbly ask.

Help us walk in paths of service
   Doing all we can
By giving thanks through kindness
   To our fellowman.

Virginia Katherine Oliver

Shining Prayer

One cannot measure warmth or love
   Nor grace of Him who reigns above,
Consideration, Mother high,
   Nor flavor from an apple pie.
The fingers, bent, on Grandma's hand
   And loving hearts that understand,

A father's toil to clothe his brood
   And set a table with such food,
The magic of a tender kiss—
   Oh, Lord, I have no words for this.
Tongue cannot speak in proper place;
   Find these on my Thanksgiving face.

Mae Baber

Treasure Bins

Old cellar bins
In the scented dark
Held orchard treasure
In days gone by,
Astrachan, Dutchess,
Winesap, Stark—
The captured essence
Of earth and sky
From springtime's bower
Of blossomed trees,
Kiss of the wind
And the balm of rain,
Wooed by the summer's
Honeybees,
Burnished where sun's caress
Had lain.
Yellow Transparent
And odd Sheep's Nose,
Baldwin succulent
Through the winter's ire
(Apple pies, dumplings,
Though cold wind blows,
And munching beside
The crackling fire).
Lift the latch
On the cellar door;
Up seeps the redolence—
Breathe it deep.
Jonathan, Wealthy,
Sweet to the core,
Safe in their bins
To winter keep.
Ben Davis, Greening,
Blue Pearmain,
McIntosh blushing
And Northern Spy—
Their remembered fragrance
Returns again
Wafted on dreams
Of the times gone by;
Fruits more precious,
By far, were these
Than the mythical apples
Of Hesperides.

Ruth B. Field

A Prayer of Thanksgiving

Almighty God, who hast given us this good land for our heritage; We humbly beseech thee that we may always prove ourselves a people mindful of thy favour and glad to do thy will. Bless our land with honourable industry, sound learning, and pure manners. Save us from violence, discord, and confusion; from pride and arrogancy, and from every evil way. Defend our liberties, and fashion into one united people the multitudes brought hither out of many kindreds and tongues. Endue with the spirit of wisdom those to whom in thy Name we entrust the authority of government, that there may be justice and peace at home, and that, through obedience to thy law, we may show forth thy praise among the nations of the earth. In the time of prosperity, fill our hearts with thankfullness, and in the day of trouble, suffer not our trust in thee to fail.

AMEN

PAUL MANN

Thanksgiving Tapestry

Special Thoughts About Thanksgiving

Pumpkin pies as yellow as gold—
Melting lusciousness untold!
Puddings, pickles, sauces various,
These to tender lads precarious!
Last of all—by no means least—
Crowning all the jolly feast,
Making all the air quite murky,
Smoked the plump and light brown turkey.

George Cooper

Best of all is it
To preserve everything
In a pure, still heart,
And let there be
For every pulse a thanksgiving
And for every breath a song.

Konrad von Gesner

Nothing is more honorable
Than a grateful heart.

Seneca

The good God bless this day,
And we forever and aye
Keep our love living
Till all men neath heaven's dome
Sing Freedom's Harvest-home
In one Thanksgiving!

Robert Bridges

In fall
November pulls
Her golden mantle close,
Then pillows her head on autumn's leaves
And sleeps.

Emily Carey Alleman

Autumn ... season of mist
and mellow fruitfulness.

John Keats

God painted all the autumn leaves
And put to sleep the flowers
And told the birds to find a place
To spend their winter hours.

Charles Bowman

Heap high the farmer's winter hoard!
Heap high the golden corn!
No richer gift has Autumn poured
From out her lavish horn.

John Greenleaf Whittier

In every thing give thanks.

1 Thessalonians 5:18

Let us give thanks to God
on Thanksgiving Day.
Nature is beautiful
and fellowmen are dear
and duty is close beside us
and God is over us
and in us.

Phillips Brooks

Gratitude is the fairest blossom
Which springs from the soul,
And the heart of man
Knoweth none more fragrant.

Hosea Ballou

You cannot hope to enjoy the harvest
without laboring in the field.

Author Unknown

We thank Thee, then, O Father,
For all things bright and good,
The seed-time and the harvest,
Our life, our health, our food.

Matthias Claudias

Gratitude takes three forms:
a feeling in the heart,
an expression in words,
and a giving in return.

Author Unknown

Gratitude is the memory of the heart.

Jean Baptiste Massieu

Think, oh, grateful, think!
How good the God of Harvest is to you;
Who pours abundance
O'er your flowing fields.

James Thomson

The bright leaves have fallen,
and late autumn has come.
On the farmlands the harvest
has been gathered in,
safe from the winter storms,
and in the roadside and city markets
the stalls are colorful
with fall fruits and vegetables.
November is the month
to appreciate and share
the bounty that is ours,
not forgetting those in want.

Esther York Burkholder

Autumn … the year's last,
loveliest smile.

Bryant

Spires

No city can be strange if there but rise
The gleam of steeples in its azure skies;
No road is foreign—gray or amber brown—
Which leads me into any distant town
If spires lift up beyond to welcome me.
Where churches are, my friends will surely be!

"A haven here, a place for peace and rest!"
These gleaming steeples to my soul attest.
"Come, worship here in sweet tranquillity!
Come, meditate!" the steeples say to me.
No city can be strange if there are spires
To mark the place of peace my soul desires.

Julia Lott

A Prayer
for
All Seasons

Our loving Creator:

How wonderful is your creation of the universe, the earth, all nature, and humanity ...

We thank you for the privilege of being a part of your creation ...

How beautiful the changing seasons ... The rebirth and new life of spring ... The warmth and generosity of summer ... The brilliant beauties and the harvesttime offerings of autumn ... And the restful, quiet grandeur of winter, the majestic season ...

We thank you for the variety, the productivity, and the serenity you bless us with in these changing seasons . . .

How boundless and abiding is your love . . . How comforting and encouraging is the love, akin to yours, of family and friends and neighbors . . . There is no boundary line separating us from a neighbor; for a neighbor may be found in any part of our whole wide world . . .

We thank you for your great love that moves and motivates our human love . . .

What a marvelous blessing it is to awaken each morning to a new day . . . Endless opportunities and possibilities come with every day . . . We especially are grateful for this precious gift . . . Help us to use it wisely . . . Amen.

Mildred Jordan

New England Heritage

Many early visitors to America were in search of adventure and precious metals and, having found both, returned to their homelands. There were many others who came in groups, anxious to throw off the yoke of tyrant rulers and to be free to live their own lifestyle and to worship the great Creator in their own way.

During the early years of the reign of the English King James, a religious group in the city of Scrooby met weekly in the home of William Brewster. They were dissenters from the established church, but the king was not in favor of their movement and caused some of them to be imprisoned and hanged. He finally allowed the group of dissenters to leave the country, and they migrated to Amsterdam, then to Leydon, Holland, where they were warmly welcomed.

It soon became evident that a continued stay in Holland would result in their children becoming Dutch and losing their English language, habits and customs, so they decided to move on. Because of their wanderings, they became known as Pilgrims.

They returned to England and obtained the permission of the king to settle in America, providing they would cause him no further trouble. With great difficulty they were able to finance and supply two small ships, the Speedwell and the Mayflower, and then started on their journey across the ocean.

Shortly after sailing, however, the Speedwell sprang a leak, so both ships returned to port. On September 6, 1620, the Mayflower sailed alone with 102 people aboard. The ocean trip was very grueling, and on November 21, 1620, they dropped anchor near present-day Provincetown, Massachusetts.

Before leaving the ship, all men aboard signed the Mayflower Compact, a code attesting to the facts that they were "still loyal to the king, but desired to plant a colony ... and, by the grace of God, frame a set of laws to govern their conduct and provide for their general good and welfare."

This was the beginning of a society known for its stern moral and religious doctrines. The Pilgrims produced blue laws designed to enforce their moral standards and practiced witch hunting. They also gave us public schools, libraries, the first college (Harvard), and an early (1640) printing press.

As we approach the Thanksgiving season, we can be thankful for this wonderful New England heritage that helped to create our great country.

Stanley Weinrich

THE SAFE ARRIVAL
"HE WHO BROUGHT US HERE SUSTAINS US STILL."

This Is the Land

This is the land they come to
When they came across the sea,
The wide plains unbroken
And the forest aisles untrod.
This is the land our fathers sought,
Longing to be free
In body and in spirit,
Free to serve and worship God.

The land they left was an old land;
The land they left was home;
But stronger than the ties of blood
And louder than the cry
Of dear insistent voices
From their own native loam
Was the calling of a new land
Beneath an alien sky.

They found the land; they conquered it;
They set one day aside
To thank their God for blessings
Far beyond their hopes and dreams;
And now, today, can we do less,
Looking down the wide
Fertile fields and valleys
Where the harvest stubble gleams?

Can we do less? Oh, may we rise
Above our doubts and fears.
God help us hold our heritage
Of strength and bravery;
We must not, dare not, lose it.
God of the fruitful years,
We thank Thee as our fathers did;
We love and worship Thee.

Grace Noll Crowell

Thanksgiving with the Pilgrims

Esther Payne Davis

If you were having Thanksgiving dinner with the Pilgrims, you would:

Feel at home in a plain, homespun dress dyed with a somber color from leaves and berries if you were a woman, or in leather breeches and leggings if you were a man.

Be served first if you were a man.

Be served by Priscilla Alden, an excellent cook.

Look across the split-log tables into the faces of ninety invited Red Men who brought five deer and oysters for the feast.

Sit on stools or logs while your Indian friends preferred to sit on the ground.

Hear the clatter of treasured pewter serving dishes on the long table. Notice the only centerpiece on the log table—a large saltcellar.

Share your twelve-inch hollowed-out wooden plate, called a trencher, with another person.

Share one of the few knives to cut your meat because forks were not yet in use.

Eat with a clamshell or wooden spoon.

Dine on wild turkey, wood pigeons, partridge, and geese brought by four men sent "fowling" by Governor Bradford.

Taste *sellery* for the first time. Learn it was brought from England as a seed, that it tastes good eaten with meat.

Nibble on dried cranberries knowing there was no sugar for jelly making.

Break wheat bread with your hosts, their first since leaving England. Only cornmeal and rye flour had been available until now.

Enjoy corn in various forms—parched or roasted, hoecake (baked on a hoe in the fireplace), ashcake (baked in the ashes).

Learn of Indian pudding, made of cornmeal and molasses boiled in a bag. Be glad the hogshead of molasses arrived in time to sweeten your Indian pudding.

Thank Squanto for showing your hosts how to prepare these succulent dishes.

Marvel that a certain kind of corn, when shaken over the coals in earthen jars, exploded into fluffy whiteness.

Have to settle for suet pudding instead of plum pudding.

Not see pumpkin pie on the bountiful table because your hosts did not know what to do with this formidable vegetable they called pompion.

Pretend not to notice that the mince pies were made with venison and dried cherries instead of raisins and beef.

Take time to watch Miles Standish march his small group of soldiers who discharged blank volleys to entertain and impress the Indian guests.

Be entertained, in turn, by the Indians displaying their prowess with the bow and arrow.

Expect to prolong and enjoy this feasting and revelry for three days.

End your Thanksgiving dinner by joining in a hymn and hearing a prayer of thanksgiving to "Almighty God for all His blessings and His divine providence which saved the colony from drought and starvation."

America

America! America!
Land ever dear to me,
Land where the Pilgrims sought retreat
And planted liberty,

Land where they conquered varied foes
Around on every hand,
And where, in spite of handicaps,
They founded this great land.

O beautiful America!
Your wonders never cease,
The beauties of both land and sea
And sweet content and peace,

The beauty of the low foothills
Beyond the fertile plain
And lofty mountains looking down
On fields of golden grain,

The mighty rivers rushing on
To join the ocean wide,
The many placid lakes and streams
That dot the countryside,

The grandeur of the forest dense
Where not a sound is heard
Except soft whispers of the trees
Or singing of a bird,

The majesty of ocean might
Whose billows surge and roar
And then in baffled fury dash
Against the rocky shore,

The tranquil peace of little towns
Nestled on every side,
With white church perched upon the hill
Where God seems to abide.

The Pilgrims planted freedom's seed,
Then nurtured its faint gleam;
Its benefits we now enjoy,
Fulfillment of their dream.

Our valiant sires for freedom fought
Midst sacrifice and pain;
They loved their country more than self
And freedom more than gain.

They overcame the tyrant's might
So their land could be free;
A priceless heritage they left—
Our land of liberty.

My beautiful America!
The great hope of the West,
How oft you've been the promised land
To the hopeless and oppressed.

Myrtie Fisher Seaverns

Fall Flowers

I love the crimson wine of autumn flowers,
As if Dame Nature saved her richest brew
For a last fling and from her storehouse drew
Flagons of amber for her parting hours.

I love chrysanthemums in rich attire,
Like royal princes of an ancient line
Decked in their purple robes of fair design,
The worthy offspring of a noble sire.

I stand in worship where an artist laid
A master brush upon a canvas rare
And painted all his richest fancy there
In colors gorgeous as an old brocade,

The warmth of cochineal, the flaming sheen
Of canna lilies in a city park,
Deep as the color of arbutus bark,
Adding their beauty to the autumn scene.

As marriage bells are to a happy bride,
So is November to the year's advance;
As music rounding out a lovely dance,
So autumn flowers bloom in conscious pride.

And in their hearts, like precious ointment poured,
The crimson wine of all the year is stored.

Edna Jaques

What Is Thanksgiving?

Thanksgiving . . . the last Thursday in November is so designated . . . cold and crisp . . . the end of fall's harvest. The day dawns early for kitchen folk, and midmorning oven aromas tarry in the room to delight the nose and tempt the appetite. The turkey grows brown and delectable, its stuffing moist and savory. Kettles steam, pies turn golden, and the table gleams with silver and crystal. Fruit bowls overflow, and the nutcracker is prominent. Guests arrive . . . a multitude of greetings expressed to one and all. And at long last, the turkey is on the platter, and the bell announces, "Dinner is served!" Not a moment too soon for the children asking first bid on the favored drumsticks. White-haired, respected Grandpa asks the blessing, little heads bow, and mature hearts thank God for fruitful days and bountiful hours, for His love and help in time of trial, for His strength in moments of grief, and for His unending care. Thanksgiving . . . the day of praise . . . of hope . . . and gratefulness. Grandpa, his mellow words steady and unwavering, closes the prayer, "Oh, God, may we live each new day in blessed deeds of thanksgiving. Amen"

Sandy Cayman

Geo. Hinke

Thanksgiving

There's an almost Christmas feeling
   In the happy time of year
When the turkey gains full stature
   As a messenger of cheer;
When plans for making merry
   Have a Yuletide flavor rare
That spreads joy throughout our valley,
   When Thanksgiving's in the air.

Now each shop and store is crowded
   With eager folk who price
Cakes and pies and turkey fixings
   Rich with condiments and spice,
And small boys dream of puddings
   As they count the hours away
Till they gather round the table
   On a glad Thanksgiving Day.

Now's the time for helping neighbors
   That their tables, too, may bear
All the bounties of God's goodness
   That are ample everywhere.
May the day be crowned with glory
   When, with everyone in place,
Heads bow low around the table
   In a fervent prayer of grace.

Brian F. King

Thanksgiving Homecoming

Thanksgiving means homecoming. Over the years, the holiday has been a succession of windswept November highways, their hard coldness promising winter storms. I remember those earlier days when I could escape the college dorm, scurrying down the stairs with a duffel bag half-full of clothes and a couple of textbooks for last-minute studying. All over campus, as the russet leaves were falling in a seasonal dance of death, there was a similar rush.

Any holiday implied freedom from the daily grind of lectures, cafeteria leftovers and late-night cramming. Thanksgiving, though, was something extra-special. It was a day perching on the frozen edge of another season. The steel-gray skies with their overhanging, grumpy clouds saw to that. Thanksgiving was a mid-semester relief, with expectations of soon-to-come Christmas. It would be a long weekend away from all the academic frenzy that marked our lives at that time—just what the doctor would order, I always believed.

Those of us who didn't have a car would line up rides with our classmates, asking, pleading, cajoling if just one more body could cram into the backseat, and help with the gas and the driving. Those lucky enough to be squeezed in would suffer through interminable hours of raucous singing and lengthy discussions about the state of the world, the latest campus fad, the best-looking girls, or the complaints about Philosophy 101.

Then there was the year I caught a ride with a vacationing family and had to hold a squealing baby. This proved to be more fun than rides with collegiate buddies. I enjoyed having these other travelers touch my life during the journey. They went out of their way to drop me off at my front door—our house was several blocks from the main highway through town. Now that was a kindness for which to be thankful.

November was always frosty, with a hint of snowflakes just over the horizon. Driving those long miles between college town and hometown provided plenty of reflection time between the songs and conversation. As the initial rush of words died down among those of us in the car, the quiet moments were welcome.

Thanksgiving—the holiday was always more than the Pilgrims and their storybook feast. Thanksgiving was eternally a pilgrimage of the heart. Even now, as I look back over those years, I see our house looming out of the November night, with the lighted windows opening to the darkened world. Excitement always built those last few miles outside of town, the last few blocks before home. From the highway, I could spot the halo from the porch light, a beacon signaling that all was well.

Warmth would be on the inside, as would foods prepared by grandmothers to chase away a semester of stomach growls. Holiday breads, pies, and jams sent their delicious advertisements far afield, capturing dreams and holding them fast. As the front door opened to the wanderer, family hugs all around solidified the Thanksgiving feeling. Frenzied tail thumping by the ancient family dog—a now-arthritic pal from grade-school days—would bring back memories.

There would be a three-steps-at-a-time run up the stairs to throw my bag into my old room. It was then back downstairs for supper and talking—always talking. The words would bounce around the warm kitchen, filling in the corners with laughter, excitement, and tall tales, with questions fired in between. Late into the night, we would converse, chatting about school, home, work, and the pheasants in the outlying cornfields.

A bathtime ritual before bed, to remove the highway grime, would involve sinking deep into hot, soapy water. The tub, up on eagle-claw feet, was a delight after weeks of showers. Properly soaped and cleansed, I could then, and only then, collapse between freshly pressed linen sheets. The next morning would usher in an official, full-blown Turkey Day with all the trimmings: cranberries, uncles, stuffing, walks around the neighborhood, cousins, pumpkin pie, aunts, and all the rest.

That's a Thanksgiving homecoming!

Martin Hintz

Happy
Thanksgiving

When Thanksgiving comes around this year ... May wondrous blessings flow ... May candles set the centerpiece ... Set faces all aglow ... And may a prayer of thanks go up ... For bounty and for good ... May every member understand ... And be happy as he should ... Take out the horn of plenty ... And make merry everywhere ... And spread your gratitude around ... And all your bounty share.

Vivian Marie Chatman

Every year around Thanksgiving
When the Honey Bowl game was played,
The good citizens of Bearbank
Held a Honey Bowl Parade.

Ted Edward Bear—Ted E. for short—
Thought building floats was fun.
He asked all his friends to help him;
They would build the grandest one.

When Ted came to ask permission,
The Grand Marshall said, and I quote,
"This parade is too important.
You're too small to have a float!"

Then Ted told Patti and Henry
They could build a great float, no doubt.
First they must learn the real meaning ...
What was Thanksgiving all about?

The Bears Find Thanksgiving

He took the wheels from his wagon,
Some boards spread with paper and paste.
He built a huge horn of plenty
And fastened it firmly in place.

Inside the horn was a table;
In plain sight for all to view
They placed a turkey and trimmings;
Three bears giving thanks were there, too.

Thanksgiving Day at last arrived.
Ted's friends brought the float to the scene.
"I said NO!" the Grand Marshall shouted.
His face was ferocious and mean.

Sadly they pushed their float uphill
So the big parade could move past.
The whistle blew! And the crowd cheered!
Ted Bear was excited at last.

Cheerleaders pleased the roaring crowd.
Marching bands stepped out in close ranks.
Floats told of honey and money—
None mentioned a time to give thanks.

The parade was almost over.
Ted's friends gave their float a push;
To their surprise it rolled downhill
And joined the parade with a rush.

Then a hush fell over the big crowd.
They recalled the very best part.
In Bearbank and the world over
Thanksgiving must come from the heart.

The big bowl game was half over.
Judges now had grown very wise.
For showing THANKSGIVING spirit,
Ted E. Bear's float had won first prize!

Alice Leedy Mason

November Enchantment

And now the hills are capped with snow;
The lanes are white on white
With milky draperies aglow
In suns of brilliant light.

The shrubs and bushes grow huge flowers
Like cotton or white lace,
And Winter tightly holds the hours
In one cold, tight embrace.

No place is like we know it now,
For snow has taken over
With canopies across each bough;
White carpets hide the clover.

The fences are a spider's bed
Of silken threads spun wide,
Each post a sentry so well fed,
A sort of soldier-guide.

And pastures boast such beauty rare;
So constant are the miles
In white, and beautiful, we dare
Believe in nature's wiles.

Enchanted by the scene we stand,
Slaves to a vivid fairyland.

Helen Loomis Linham

A Feeling of Thankfulness

Milt Heitzman

It was eleven o'clock on that Thanksgiving morning. Our car scrunched over the loose gravel, down the narrow winding road, onto the parking area of Montauk Point, Long Island, New York. We could see the Montauk lighthouse not far away. When we looked out to the east over the beach, we saw the cold, steel gray of the sea. We imagined the Pilgrim ship approaching. Truly this was a stern and rockbound coast this Thanksgiving Day. But was this a good spot for the family feast? Would our children accept this kind of celebration on a family holiday?

About a week before, our family was bemoaning the fact that we now lived eight hundred miles away from the rest of our family and that Thanksgiving Day, instead of being a celebration around the festive table in Illinois, would be rather limited for the four of us—myself, my wife, our eleven-year-old son, Jack, and our thirteen-year-old daughter, Julie. It was our first year in the East, and we sometimes felt lonely.

As our young ones complained that week about the way the food was cooked; what a terrible school they attended; and "why did we have to come out here anyway?" both of us parents came to the same thought at the same time. Perhaps we could create a special Thanksgiving observance—maybe we could even pattern it upon the original one. Wouldn't that be something!

What if we could have a meal like the first Thanksgiving meal? Could we imagine how they lived so long ago? And from there, our plan developed.

It was a secret plan. Thanksgiving would be celebrated at a lonely spot. We would have a picnic, bring the food, and cook it over fire. We would impress upon our children's hearts an appreciation for the life that they enjoy. One reason we kept all of this secret was that we did not want to face the negative campaign we expected would come from the youthful part of our family if they knew everything ahead of time.

So we parents furtively studied the map. Should we go to a national park in Virginia? No, too far. Should we go to Mystic, Connecticut? It was historical and was on the seacoast like the Pilgrims' settlement, but it was quite a distance away and we learned that it was closed on Thanksgiving.

Where should we go?

And then as we looked at the map of New York and especially Long Island, where we lived, our eyes and thoughts traveled east. Montauk Point, a spit of land stretching out into the Atlantic Ocean and marked only by a protective light to warn the passing ships; yes, we would try it! And then we saw on a detailed map that there was a picnic ground in a small park there. Just right! But not one word to the younger generation; we would go on this Pilgrim journey with only the message: we are going east!

The day before Thanksgiving was the usual busy time, preparing the turkey and the rest of the food on the menu. The house was filled with the aroma of the cooking turkey; dressing was made; gravy was prepared. This was really going to be a different sort of picnic.

Then the day came. We all climbed into the car, including Rinny our dog, and we headed east. We drove from the urban sprawl of Nassau County and past the newly built homes in western Suffolk County. We continued going east on the road called Montauk Highway.

The farther we went, the more isolated and lonely the countryside seemed to be until we came to the Hamptons. Long known for their wealthy residents and summer activities, the

Hamptons seemed to signal that this was now the end of twentieth-century America. Now we were entering the land of the Pilgrims. To underline that thought, we passed the Shinnecock Indian Reservation.

There, decades long gone, a group of Americans had marked off the boundaries for other Americans. Should we invite them to the Thanksgiving feast too? No, we did not know them; they did not know us. We were strangers in a lonely land, and our isolated car traveled on.

As we drove through the hamlet of Montauk, a real feeling of expectation came over us. We were about to arrive at the end of Long Island, and the next body of land east of us was England itself—the original home of the Pilgrims.

As we turned a small curve, we looked and there was the Montauk lighthouse on a high point and beneath it, some distance away, was a parking lot and the picnic ground. "How will the kids take this?" I said to myself.

If this had been a summer trip, we would have had crowds of people milling around us. We would have eased our car into a row of parked cars, and we would have had to rush for a vacant table in the picnic ground. But now we were alone. As the car doors slammed and seemed to echo in the stillness, only the wind spoke back. We watched our dog take off at full speed and realized we were truly alone. There was no park attendant to remind us to have the dog on a leash. There was no one to tell us where to build our campfire—in fact, there was no one except ourselves to know that we had a fire in our small charcoal burner.

This was indeed Thanksgiving. The wind, the cold, and the bleakness established a certain strength and beauty that made us realize that our forefathers were a strong, hearty lot.

We lit the fire. Paper, charcoal, lighter fluid, and matches. We were generations away from the original reality. Only in our imaginations could we know the true thankful spirit of those Pilgrims.

The young people and the dog took off for the nearby shore. They clambered on the rocks, went close to the lighthouse, and ran along the beach. Meanwhile, we heated the Thanksgiving meal.

The turkey slices were put into a saucepan with the previously prepared gravy; the par-tially baked potatoes were wrapped in aluminum foil, and the ears of preboiled corn were wrapped as well. All was placed over the charcoal fire, and my wife and I sat back to enjoy the isolation.

Across America, families were going over the hills and through the woods to Grandmother's house. Even in Illinois, our own families were getting together and talking about the crops and how big the turkey was and whether or not the boys would bring in some rabbits from their hunting trip. But we were here on the edge of our nation and the edge of history.

Here we could actually feel the fear, the faith, and the hope of Captain Miles Standish, Priscilla and John Alden.

Many had died in that first year at the Plymouth settlement so long ago. It was only a few hundred miles from where we prepared to eat our own Thanksgiving meal. Now those ancestors seemed alive. The new land had blessed them; they were free to worship and give thanks.

For our little family this was the moment of truth. We would know whether the experiment was good or was a failure. The meal was ready.

"Julie! Jack! Rinny! Come, come," I called.

We sat around the park picnic table, joined hands, and bowed our heads. Each one said his own prayer.

"Thank You, God, for giving us this place, this country where we can have food and family and a future. Thank You, God, for giving us this freedom to worship You out here on this point of land so far from, and yet so close to, our loved ones and to You," I said.

"Thank You for this day," said Jack.

Then Julie said, "Thank You for letting us know and understand the Pilgrims better."

My wife closed our individual thanks with, "Thank You for our family here, and in Illinois." Then we all said together, "Thank You, God."

Years later, our daughter, now a mother herself, when writing of her most memorable Thanksgiving, described our Montauk Thanksgiving picnic. She told of the bayberries, the deer dashing into the thicket back of the park, and the shells and pieces of driftwood admired during the walk along the beach. "Best of all," she wrote, "was the feeling of thankfulness for our loving family and our wonderful country."

Never Bereft of Loveliness

The flamboyant colors of October
Have given way to more subdued tones
Of old rose, bronze, and russet; even these
Will soon be no more. But brown pinecones,
The scarlet berries of pyracanthas,
And silver plumes of grasses will be left
To attract our nature-loving eyes.
We know that we shall never be bereft
Of loveliness, no matter what the season
Might be; even though the death-dealing kiss
Of winter touch November's countryside—
We have the Creator to thank for this!

Earle J. Grant

Vision

The last crisp leaf has fallen from the oak tree,
And across November fields the eye sees far.
The woodland boughs are only lacework patterns
And offer to the view no leafy bar
Except for here and there a nest abandoned.
Now is the time to see the distant ridge
Dark with spruce against a lilac skyline,
A shining creek, a stalwart wooden bridge
That looks much like a quaint old covered wagon,
Or still, perhaps, a house beneath tall pines,
Its friendly woodsmoke trailing from the chimney,
Its windows wide through which warm lamplight shines.

And it would seem that there must be a time
For man to see the realm of life that lies
In distances beyond the obvious—
A clear perspective with far-reaching eyes.

Florence Marie Taylor

November Days

November and the days are gray;
The trees are stark and bare;
The autumn leaves are fast asleep;
Scent of winter is in the air.

The earth is still, her time of rest,
Her generous bounty in store;
Sleep on, thou weary one, sleep on,
And take thy rest once more.

The lake forsaken, the waters chill
Reflecting the gray of the sky;
The cottages shuttered, their chimneys cold,
The small canoes high and dry,

The air is still; no voices call.
The deer come forth to the brink;
They lift their heads and sniff the air
Before they come forth to drink.

The earth lies hushed and waiting,
O'er the landscape a smoky haze;
A hint of snow is in the air,
For these are November days.

Naomi I. Parks

Days of Fall

The days are growing shorter, capped by chilly nights.
Ducks among the cattails prepare for southward flights.
Colored leaves are falling; their journey now begins
To unknown destinations when caught by restless winds.

Squirrels are mighty busy, working hard all day,
Gathering winter food supplies—no time now to play.
Chipmunks, in their burrows, prepare for winter sleep,
While playful deer and bunnies swiftly run and leap.

Ernest Jack Sharpe

I Found the Wintertime

I found the wintertime today
Along the wondrous autumn way.
The very lovely snowflakes white
Had softly fallen in the night;
Each naked branch now glistened fair
Within the frosty morning air.

How silent are the magic charms
As Winter holds us in his arms,
An artistry just God can bring,
A miracle in everything.
So thick and deep snow's carpet lies
In wintertime's so sweet surprise.

The country lanes did bid me go
Into a world of sparkling snow,
A loveliness as yet untold
That glistened neath the sunshine gold
To ever thrill this heart of mine.
Today I found the wintertime.

                    Garnett Ann Schultz

COLOR ART AND PHOTO CREDITS
(in order of appearance)

Front and back cover, Freelance Photographers Guild; inside front cover, Fred Sieb; Taftsville Covered Bridge, Taftsville, Vermont, Eric Sanford; Chrysanthemums, Hampfler Studios; Peaceful valley, Hampfler Studios; Fresh fruits, Alpha Photo Associates; Kitchen corner, Three Lions, Inc.; Grapes from Napa Valley Vineyard, David Ryan; Colorful Oley Valley, Pennsylvania, Hampfler Studios; Winding road near Reading, Vermont, Josiah Davidson; Color in the country, H. Armstrong Roberts; Bounteous yield, H. Armstrong Roberts; Holiday fun, Bob Taylor; Paring apples, Bob Taylor; A PRAYER OF THANKSGIVING, Paul Mann, photo by Gerald Koser; Village in autumn, Fred Sieb; LANDING OF THE PILGRIMS, Harold M. Lambert; Thanksgiving fare from Plimoth Plantation, Plymouth, Massachusetts, Fred M. Dole; Fall flowers, H. Armstrong Roberts; THANKSGIVING BIRD, George Hinke, photo by Gerald Koser; The spirit of Thanksgiving, Bob Taylor; THE BEARS FIND THANKSGIVING, Rick Reinert, photo by Gerald Koser; First snowfall, Eric Sanford; Autumn stream, Vermont, H. Armstrong Roberts; Colorful rain barrel, Fred M. Dole; Autumn leaves, Gene Ahrens; Ice covering European Cranberry, Hampfler Studios; inside back cover, H. Armstrong Roberts.

ACKNOWLEDGMENTS

NOW WINTER COMES (In fall November pulls . . .) by Emily Carey Alleman. From her book: THE GYPSY HEART, Copyright 1957 by Emily Carey Alleman. This poem was previously published in THE CHRISTIAN SCIENCE MONITOR. Reprinted with permission of the author. THE INDISCREET CHRYSANTHEMUMS by Dorothy Bettencourt Elfstrom. From her book: CHALLENGE OF THE SEASONS, Copyright © 1963 by Dorothy Bettencourt Elfstrom. Reprinted with her permission. ON THIS DAY OF THANKSGIVING by Lansing Christman. From A HILLSIDE HARVEST by Lansing Christman, Copyright © 1957 by Lansing Christman and the Taylor-Powell Press. THIS IS THE LAND by Grace Noll Crowell. Used by permission of the Estate of Grace Noll Crowell. NEVER BEREFT OF LOVELINESS by Earle J. Grant. Previously published in DAILY MEDITATION. Reprinted with permission of the author. AUTUMN COLORS by Polly Perkins. From her book: SILHOUETTES AND SAMPLERS, Copyright © 1959 by Dorrance & Company.

Home for the Holidays . . .

As your home sparkles with the warmth and magic of Christmas, plan to remember your family and friends with subscriptions to Ideals.

Begin your subscription with the upcoming Christmas Issue, the 38th season for this beautiful publication. Open the cover of *Christmas Ideals* and step into the magical Christmastime of Germany or accompany St. Nicholas on his rounds through the legend of his very first trip. Norman Rockwell's painting will remind you of Christmases past; and the lavish illustrations and simple, yet timeless Biblical passages will remind you of the significance of Christmas.

Let the joy and love of the Christmas season reach from your home to the homes of your friends with a gift subscription to Ideals. This Christmas spirit will continue year round as your friends receive their beautiful Ideals issues. There's no lovelier way to say "We care about you!"

The warmth and magic of Christmas will continue in your home, too, with your very own Ideals subscription. As winter gives way to spring, let Ideals welcome the changing seasons, each with its own delightful sparkle and wonder.

Ideals has become a tradition in thousands of homes. This year, bring Ideals home for the holidays—eight times a year.